FOR
HORSE
LOVERS

A POCKET BOOK OF POEMS

Zoë Coade

Published by
Zoë Coade, the Netherlands

Contact via website:

ZOECOADE.COM/BOOKS

Cover artwork by Zoë Coade
Photo front page: Cassie Tooms
Photo back page: Mirjam van Eck

First edition
ISBN 978-90-826145-4-1

For the horses, a voice.

Preface

Simply put, I was inspired to write these poems and share some messages that I believe are not just important for me but also for our friend the horse. This anthology is a representation of my thoughts and personal experiences, from past to present day as a Horse Professional, Instructor and Influencer.

As we all know, social media has fast become a place where if one is brave enough to express opinions, one can expect to receive them back.

I find this provides minimal help. Especially if you are looking to support change in areas that are ethically incorrect when there *are* other options. Unruly comments tend to take over the original content, so I wanted to create a platform that is stronger than that.

At the time of writing this book and for some forty years already; I have housed my horses at a very busy stable where my day-to-day affairs are very different to that of somebody who houses their horses in a private residence.
I have no privacy.
Neither do most my students.

I also see a lot that can improve ethically.

Limited in my vocabulary, I am no PhD student of the English language and speak only from the heart. I am very proud of my work and storytelling. I recommend reading all of the poetry where one can feel the balance of the messages depicted in different poetic writing styles.
The subjects are presented in no particular order, only alphabetical.

The idea is not to offend the enthusiastic reader, although one can't help know in advance that this will not be avoided. If one does indeed find themselves displeased, then I can only encourage them to search deep as to why that happened!
After all, these truths are my truths; what are your truths?

If all readers find at least a few of my poems enlightening, then I believe I did my job well.

In closing, some of the messages may seem repetitive in their content; this is because the value and the meaning behind them mean a great deal. I know and witness everyday how important it is for the people and how much more dignified situations can become for the horses when their humans know there are other ways to train and be with them.

As true horse lovers, let's add years to the horse's lives rather than take them away and while we do that, find a way to preserve their pride in which they so rightly deserve.

Let us all be a voice for them, the horses.

Preface poem

Equine welfare,
how can one help diffuse,
trolling and b*tching,
no remedy for such *abuse!*

Here I share some messages
conveyed another way,
amplifying simple knowledge,
of what I want to say!

Maybe only one poem
will sit well with you,
I hope for the rest at least,
more than just a few.

My aim is to compliment
what you already know,
by demonstrating my passion
and reaping what I sow.

Lest not forget the instrument
of these communications,
the horses and the ponies,
a friend, a servant of all the *nations.*

A desperate Horse's Plea

I see you,
do you see me?
I hear you,
do you hear me?

I try very hard
to understand,
the confusing touch
of your human hand!

I don't want to resist,
but sometimes that's how I feel,
your energy, your presence,
it's not always the best deal.

There are other days;
it all feels so very pleasant,
in the now, in the moment
and in the *present!*

Please may I ask,
since it was you that chose me,
to give me more time for stuff,
it works wait and see.

I love to learn new things,
but show me slow and right,
I do not speak your language,
I may fright or flight.

If you can promise this,
other things I can forget,
don't be hard on me or yourself,
no need to get upset.

We are two different species,
I want to learn and love man,
can you really return the loyalty,
I'm pretty sure you can.

I hear you,
I hope now you hear me!
I see you,
I hope now you see me!

A good Horse(wo)man

A good Horse(wo)man has a gift,
the horse is always right,
their ego never cheats them,
by using flight or fight.

They know how to prepare them,
so they feel like superstars,
rather than break and belittle them
and create unwanted scars.

They always have a plan,
are flexible when required,
not running them to a point,
of being exhausted and super tired!

Their feet and hands are soft,
they work independent and together,
never do they restrict their movement,
with needless straps of *leather!*

They know the perfect moment
to set things up real well,
by not assuming they remember yesterday
and put the horse through living hell.

Their timing and experience is precise
and nobody should compare,
you know them when you see them,
because their knowledge they will share.

Always

Breath down my neck,
shivers down my spine,
these moments with you,
life is really fine.

Your eyes draw me in,
I feel so secure,
innocent and protective,
a heart that is so pure.

Thank you my friend,
you feed my heart, soul and fire,
my love for you my horse,
will never ever, tire or expire!

Autumn

A favourite season,
for me anyhow,
as trees show off their colours;
it's always a wow!

The horses are ready,
the summer was very harsh,
their coats start to flourish,
so they can cope until *March*.

The days begin to shorten,
less of them in the light I see,
no concern for them,
they have better vision than me.

As the sky gradually changes
from a blue to white and grey,
the horses mind not so much,
they just need shelter and good hay.

As winter closes in,
I do not let the weather control my time,
with good care and attention,
my horses and me, we do just *fine*.

Barn ~~b*tches~~ witches

The sourness,
the spitefulness,
those darn barn witches!
What's missing
in your life so bad,
to make you into such *b*tches?*

Fear not,
we will not lower ourselves,
to such a negative reaction.
We would not dream,
of giving any of you,
the bloody *satisfaction.*

Guess what,
we are not going anywhere,
you had better hold on!
We will carry on doing
what we are doing,
coz we're having too much *fun.*

Believe

How can your horse believe in you?
If you do not believe in yourself!
It takes confidence to create a partnership,
in return, your gift is infinite wealth.

Birth

She proudly gives birth
when your body is ready,
nature calls helping you,
to your feet fast and steady.

Your hooves are soft
so as not to damage her womb,
as your body strengthens
they harden pretty *soon.*

Your instinct gives a whisper
in a new hearing ear,
to find your next life line
of milk for a year.

As you find your balance,
your curiosity appears,
you discover your surroundings,
sometimes arousing your fears.

But your dam is your teacher;
she keeps a watchful eye,
you have so much to discover,
from the canter to the fly.

Don't worry little one,
she will protect you well and good,
keeping you safe from harm's way,
until all is understood.

As you grow in stature
you can gallop by her side,
learning how to run and buck
and be balanced in your stride.

Bonding

They *do* have emotions,
just different to you and I,
only they cannot laugh out loud,
or use tears when they cry.

But one thing they have,
that we can absolutely share,
is a feeling of love,
where in their own way they *do* care.

I believe that is why,
we can have a partnership with them,
easily broken but their kind nature
allows us to mend it *again!*

A horse does not hold grudges;
they just do what feels right,
whereas man does hold grudges
and can't resist a good fight.

The horse is very honest,
not in it to make life difficult,
any problem with them is man-made
and entirely not their *fault*.

When they chose you,
a special feeling, I can find no word,
a piece of your heart is stolen,
not hired nor is it *borrowed*.

All family of the Equidae
are so impartial, pure and sincere,
depending on their human,
they can bond in a day, maybe a year.

They can help you confront yourself,
would you want to bond with you?
When you find the true answer,
your horse will bond with you too.

Death

I was there by your side,
when you took your last breath,
the pain of you leaving us to mourn
your beautiful life and then your death,
it was simply gut wrenching,
I found it hard to tolerate,
it filled my heart with sadness,
love, dread and hate.

Although I am certain
that once again we will meet,
I know forever from that moment,
life's wonder will be complete.

Easy-boy

A poem for a friend.

Easy boy,
that's actually his real name,
first meeting a wild nature,
one could say, barely tame.

Low in confidence,
he would spook at his own fart,
but always trying to connect,
so it was there he won her *heart.*

Starting from scratch,
she built a new world for the boy,
from ground skills to riding
and playing with *the* odd toy!

Not every day is perfect,
but he always does his best,
he is learning that relaxation
is much better than tension or *stress.*

My dear friends I can't wait
to see you both in a year or three,
Saskia keep doing what you are doing,
you were meant to be.

Expectations

For the most part expectations
are way too high,
minimal practice, no patience,
some people presume to reach the sky.

There are a sombre few,
who feel they had some success,
that one time, with that one horse,
no more and no *less!*

Pretty soon they discover
it was a fluke, good luck or a gift,
spirits are low, the horse's dignity is tested
and everybody is *pissed.*

No need to be this way my dear,
please don't think yourself so special,
maybe it is time to acknowledge,
you were probably never really at that *level.*

How about you admit defeat
and set a good and truthful goal,
then when success comes your way,
you know you earned it, body, mind and soul.

Forgive me

As I run my hand,
across your soft face,
I ask please don't ever
think me a disgrace.
I do make mistakes
but I try to learn each day,
too become my best for you
in each and every way.
Your thoughts and your feelings
are all I think about,
who you are, what you do,
it really does *count.*
I ask for your forgiveness
because you *are* to me,
the most beautiful horse
I ever did see.
Although your choice is limited
and you cannot roam free,
I promise to love you forever,
because you saved me.

Heel to Toe

Grateful of my decision
to go barefoot,
supported sometimes
by the help of a rubber *boot!*

A delicate job
is that of a trimmer,
maintaining the hoof,
with a rasp, knife and nipper!

Their knowledge is broad
or at least it should be,
advising the client,
in the hope that they agree.

They only have my horses
care in mind,
in addition extra knowledge
I will always find.

Exercise, diet and the environment
the horse lives in,
all contribute to the trimmer's efforts
where good hooves we can win.

Much advice is on the market,
sometimes it's difficult to decide,
I asked those around me who were successful,
what they have tried!

Proud that my horse can walk freely,
heel to toe,
every step leading to health
and a good blood flow!

Thank you dear trimmer
for helping me and my horse,
your expertise is much appreciated,
you are a great resource.

Horse Lovers

The genuine horse lover,
another type of breed,
can't help themselves;
rambling on about their steed!

Every family member,
good friend or passer-by,
can tell of the addiction,
by just a glimpse of an eye!

Observation of the clothes they wear,
not your regular outfit,
sometimes hay decorates their hair
and their boots reek of horse *sh*t!*

Horse Lover's Emergency

'Quick' I say, '
there is a catastrophe!'
'We are head over heels obsessed,
can't you see?'

From morning to night,
we ponder about them all day,
no matter what the conversation,
it surely swings that way.

Horses and ponies,
donkeys and mules,
some would say how silly,
what mindless *fools!*

We just smile and continue
about it anyway,
be prepared, the infatuation,
it governs *everything* we say.

These animals make us happy;
they consummate our mortal soul,
*'It's an emergency, we are horse lovers
and it's out of our control!'*

I dream of horses…

I wonder
in my pensive bubble,
life with them,
never have I trouble.

Mediating a path,
I yearn to walk,
listening intently,
hoping to hear them talk.

My self-esteem and self-worth
are equally divided,
in the horse it is determined
because in them I have *confided.*

They speak only the truth,
these irreproachable beings,
they delete all pessimism
and awaken inspired *feelings!*

Captivated,
therefore I dream only of horses,
a force majeure assigned
by unknown forces.

Just

Am I not just?
The horse is.
Perhaps I am not just,
but then who is?

Am I not just?
The horse is.
I am not just,
it just is.

La Garrocha

Sharp silhouette with his vaquero hat
and sweat trickling down his cheek,
the long pole is held like a lover in his hands,
splendid at first glance, a distinct *mystique.*

His Iberian horse knows his job very well
and is connected with unsurpassed pride,
devoted to listen to his master,
for every change and given stride.

Sometimes they charge as if one spirit,
or dance around in a pirouette on the spot,
both elegant, mimicking the fight of the bull,
giving it everything that they have got.

When the ride and game is finally over,
he drops the reins for his faithful friend,
a signal that their time has ended,
no more livestock to *pretend* to defend.

Legend

Every horses potential
is vastly tremendous.
Young, old, loved or abused,
almighty and *stupendous.*

An animal so different in comparison,
somehow compelled us.
A legend that influenced unicorns
and the marvellous *Pegasus!*

Lightness

To teach a horse lightness,
we must show them what it looks like first;
'Well how do you do that?'
I hear the people say in *outburst!*

The secret is to understand your influence
at any given time,
when you approach, whilst riding them
or standing by their *side.*

A horse will always do,
what they think they are supposed to do,
everything else is for safety and comfort
or perhaps to get away from you.

If the horse is understood well
and not treated like a human,
it is possible to succeed together,
no matter what the day or *season.*

If you grab them and pull them
and just push them around,
that's what you teach them my dear,
so how can true lightness be found?

Learn to touch, lead and guide them
with an open and soft hand,
then release on the new lightness,
you may find you don't need *sound*.

Invest in your education;
everybody at least knows something,
you have nothing to lose,
only a horse, whose heart you can win.

Listen

Silent, their world,
a neigh, consternation.

Silence, just observe,
a blow out, equanimity.

Still, propensity,
a squeal, deterrent.

Stillness, restraint,
a voice, not-mandatory.

Marvellous

The outside of a horse
resembles power,
the inside of a horse
is delicate like a flower.

Once a predator
and now a herbivore,
designed to live
for many years more!

Agile in their step,
0 to 50 in a few seconds,
built in alarm to flee,
they have no *weapons*.

If they do decide to fight,
teeth and hooves will be used,
any victim of them,
will *certainly* feel abused.

One can only feel privileged
if a friend in them we make,
these marvellous animals,
a true relationship you can't fake.

Mia

Poem in reference to Zoë's award winning book
www.thehorsethatbroketwolegs.com.

My beautiful friend, my Mia,
I've known you half my life,
a big change meant we had to move,
just before you turned the age of *five.*

Our relationship took a turn for the worse,
less time for you I had,
as the days and months passed by,
I grew frightened of you and sad.

But then one day I decided,
to make a change and win back your heart,
it was not easy learning on my own,
but we made a progressive start.

A few years later and for you,
I was already a much better friend,
but in 2013 something happened,
a day I thought your life would end.

You broke a bone in your left hind leg,
snapping four places at the knee,
there was no blood or bone sticking out,
but the way you moved you could see.

My big dear friend, I could not give up,
we decided to give you a chance,
I knew one day, if I gave you time,
once again I would see you dance.

One year later all was well
and you healed mostly by yourself,
we were all so very delighted
to see you back in reasonable *health.*

As we started movement again,
you did not look quite right.
another visit to the doctor,
gave us all quite the alarming fright.

A second fracture was discovered
in your right front leg,
from balancing your weight so hard,
you cracked it like an egg.

Not all was lost just yet,
a sign you needed more time,
a few months more of love and care
and you turned out to be just fine.

To this day I am so proud of you,
everything was so worthwhile,
you bring happiness and joy to many,
one *cannot* help but *smile.*

You are more than just a friend to me,
you are my rock, my heart, my soul,
every day I get to spend with you,
makes living feel more whole.

Your mind strength and will to survive
must only be commended,
you were the one who always knew inside,
your life was far from ended.

So here we are each day a gift,
19 years old and strong,
I hope you stay the same time again;
you deserve so badly to live life long.

More beautiful than…

A pose,
more beautiful than a rose.

A stare,
more beautiful than a sun glare.

A stance,
more beautiful than a dance.

A grace,
more beautiful than a royal lace.

A love,
more beautiful than a dove.

A presence,
more beautiful than heaven.

A subsistence,
Horse, I am blessed at your existence.

My horse & hound

'Up front' I say,
without looking she goes,
keeping a good distance,
my horse *follows.*

When we arrive at a turn,
the hound gets left behind,
my horse and I continue,
interesting smells and holes to find!

I don't have to look back,
I call her name,
she runs at high speed,
thinks it's all a great game.

My Mare

She burst through the seams,
full rush to my heart,
all rust melted away,
a new life was to start.

Diamonds and gold,
could fill my pockets dearly,
I would exchange them in a beat,
for her love *sincerely*.

Only black or white,
no time for cloudy grey,
forget that and she will
have something to say.

Power and strength,
honour and noble virtue,
win her devotion and her mind
and she will take care of you.

Not today

It's the end of the day,
I bury my face in your neck,
I'm tired, been helping other horses,
my body feels like a car wreck.

I'm so sorry my friend,
we will play together another day,
when me energy is revitalised,
I can give you hundred percent all the way.

Perfect are they

Eye and mane,
a brain that's sane,
living in vain,
maybe they are *tame.*

Soft fur and nose,
always warm and close,
stature so grandiose,
a girl's over-dose!

Strong leg and hoof,
turn on a dime...poof,
from the sound of a woof,
or perhaps a *piaffe!*

No words can relay,
white, brown or bay,
night and day,
perfect are they.

Silence between the Notes

I breathe
He breathes
I blink
He blinks
I think of him
He might think of me
I stroke his neck
He might feel the stroke
I listen
He might be listening too
I try to be in the moment
He is in the moment
I want to be the silence between his notes
He is the silence between the notes

Since always

My Little Pony and
all the horses of Barbie,
Cindy too,
everything *gee-gee!*

Plastic cups for hooves,
on my hands and knees,
or a hobbyhorse,
for hours this would please.

Riding a bike,
in rising trot,
reins made of string,
more often than not.

Walls covered in posters,
Horse and Pony Magazine,
from stickers to pencil case,
oh how often I would *dream!*

One day it happened,
my folks bought me a pony,
no prouder girl in the world,
out with the fake and *phoney*.

So it is to this day,
my love is still real,
no boy or fashion ever in the way,
my heart forever they will steal!

Some

Some like to ride 'em
til the saddle blanket is wet
Some like to ride 'em
til their body breaks to a sweat

Some like to lock 'em in a corner
to mount on their back
Some like to hop-hop along
to get on 'em for that hack

Some like to wear gadgets
to make 'em do something
Some like to spur and whip 'em
to create that extra sting

Some like to lunge 'em
mostly to the left
Some like to chase 'em
until their energy is *supressed*

Some do not bother
with any of that crap
Some do not need a tie down
or a nasty chin strap

Some admit defeat
and look the horse in the eye
Some concede they want
to see 'em smile never cry

Some bite the bullet
and search a new and better way
Some don't bother
what the other people do or say

Some set the relationship
with the horse as primary
Some heed that just understanding 'em
is the *golden key*

Speed

Not much go,
a lot of whoa,
will test what you know,
usually labelled slow!

Can't stand still,
a lot of thrill,
will test your good will,
usually labelled *Crazy-Ville!*

A good balance of both,
most would loathe,
will test your own growth,
usually labelled *treasure-trove!*

Spring

The air has not quite changed just yet,
but the day time provides more light.
The birds sound different in the trees,
for sure Mother Nature is always right.

Your hair and skin start to get itchy;
because the shedding has just begun!
Tickle here, tickle there all day long,
I imagine it's not much fun.

Don't fret my horse, I will help you
and brush away the mass.
to reveal your new summer coat
as we smell the fresh meadow *grass.*

Stop

Kick 'em to go,
pull 'em to stop,
if you love them so much,
don't use that crop.
There are kinder ways
to ride and train horses,
on a trail, in the arena
and *even* on the race courses!
The change must start
with you alone,
ask for help or search
the net on your phone.
Be inspired and seek greatness,
choose who you want to be,
ask yourself are you a good teacher
and someone your horse likes to see.
Don't think for a minute
the horse does not mind,
it really is quite ignorant,
old fashioned and unkind.
So in closing, I guess
what I really want to say and express,
is to seek knowledge, drop your ego
and remember more is less.

Summer

Buzz of flies,
horse smell,
Blackbird cries,
church bell!

Cracked ground,
parched grass,
skin browned,
pain in the *ass*.

Peace at night,
un-rest in the day,
mosquitos to fight,
relentless sun-ray.

Summer is hear,
don't long for winter,
it will reappear,
like a nasty splinter.

Best memories like
swimming in the lake,
galloping freely,
many photo's to make.

Surprised

I am often baffled as to *how*
horse owners can be so surprised,
when good horsemanship is executed
and certain things are *realised*.

It surely went so well because,
more knowledge they have now got,
a new training tip is much better
than any result where they had not.

The first time they ride that young horse
or ask an older one to back-up,
it works in the first instance and well,
because of a language and clear *set-up!*

Sometimes it is something,
they have been struggling with for years,
the usual response of an unhappy horse
that might kick, bite or pin its ears.

There are so many answers;
it only improves when they open their mind,
with real solutions and having fun again,
many more surprises in return they can find.

Temptation

It's tempting to take short cuts,
plus the temptation to want too much!
Please for the horses sake ask yourself,
what gives you the right to ask as such?

That stupid Carrot Stick

'Oh that's stupid carrot stick!'
I hear some people say;
'So long and big and heavy,
I will use a whip instead, okay?'

Aware it's just information they need,
to learn the purpose of that stick,
one thing is for certain they need to know,
it is not the same as a crop or *whip*.

It's interesting how some experts
and horse professionals in the field,
turn down a tool so useful,
which can teach horses easily how to yield.

A whip encourages people to punish,
the stick they still could, but less so,
when understood how to be used correctly,
even the slowest horse can learn to go.

The stick represents many things,
it can also teach horses to be confident,
it can also help the human send a horse,
that behaves unduly *dominant*.

You see that stupid carrot stick,
it was not designed for nothing,
many horses are trained successfully using it,
which must account for something.

The Arena

When I ride my horse,
my troubles disappear,
I don't need a fancy saddle
or any special kind of gear.

The school or the arena
is a place that should be fun,
minimum pressure, no resistance,
no medal to be won!

I fear it's not the same
for other riders and their horse,
too much seriousness, misunderstanding
and unnecessary force!

It honestly and respectably,
does not have to be that way,
poor horses if you listen,
what do they actually and really say?

So the next time you are in the arena
and it feels like death warmed up,
make sure it's them, not you;
don't join the *a-hole club.*

The Art

The power, the secret,
the beauty and the glory,
is the lowering of the haunch at the hip,
hock and the *knee!*

Gymnastics in abundance,
clarified with tiny releases,
taking years to perfect,
explaining all the different pieces.

A king's horse in the making,
stallion, gelding or mare,
proud, elegant and educated,
where one *can't* help but stare!

Smooth muscles well formed,
dominate their body,
years of practice and study,
it is more than just a *hobby.*

Simply the leather straps and sticks
aid in the shape,
done well with love and kindness,
a majestic language you can *create.*

Regal in their steps and strides,
their presence is electric,
too often copies and fakes are produced
to feed the *egocentric.*

Through bending of their body and joints,
they become a master of yoga,
both in standstill and forwards,
solid top-line under and *over!*

No need to drive the horse to a place
where sweat is dripping from the chest,
to the point of being tormented,
abused and badly in need of rest.

Fitness and muscle memory
can be built-in slowly every day,
eventually it feels so easy;
the horse thinks it's time to play.

A variety of these manoeuvres
replicate the war-horse,
executed quintessentially;
a silent language without trauma, or force.

The Beach

There was one time,
I will always remember,
an icy cold day
with high wind in *November!*

As we arrived at the beach,
the chill raced down my neck,
my first thought was to turn back,
but then what the heck!

Despite the winds screaming
and whipping at us and the sea,
there was an irrefutable silence
surrounding my horse, and me.

It was like a scene from the movie;
the Lord of the Rings,
the sand danced like a mist
to the height of our *knees.*

The sky was bright blue
and the ocean a dark grey,
as the waves smashed the shore,
it washed all debris away.

I rode a few kilometres
mesmerised in some state of trance,
the cold was quickly forgotten
as if the sun was about to dance.

My horse mirrored this feeling
as if enjoying the tranquillity too,
walking slow *but* hard in the sand storm,
we were focused on riding through.

Via a path we exited the beach;
an eerie stillness befell our ears,
the dunes protection was inevitable,
like it had done for many years.

The Equus

Best International Poem Winnie Award Winner
at the EQUUS Film Festival 2018.

Choice and a destiny,
something on their mind,
the usual resolution
or a prisoner *confined.*

Snow, rain or thunder,
shut in, cannot be outside,
trapped and frightened,
or man whipping at their side.

Angelic and innocent,
things not easily forgot,
comfortable living
or their soul and mind left to rot.

Fear and mechanics,
broke their beauty for many years,
if dare resist, only hit harder,
confirming their many fears.

A servant and companion
for mankind all these centuries,
yet subject to relentless cruelty,
like the land, sea and *trees.*

Stop, look and listen,
what are they trying to say?
Perhaps a simple question
of safety, comfort, food and play!

There are a special few,
who listen to their souls,
understanding their nature,
as adults and young foals.

A promise of a language,
both can try to understand,
no punishment required,
a mutual respect of a *command.*

Time is all that is needed,
to get things good and right,
or the same thing is done over and over,
resulting in a fight.

Look at their ears, in their eyes,
hear them breathe and sigh,
man has started to change their method
and ask how and why.

They have survived the ice age,
roamed our earth for so long,
a question of what we love about them,
where did it all go wrong.

A chief would ride in full gallop,
shooting arrows from their back,
how was this possible in the open prairie,
no whip, spur or tack?

Caring for their young,
not weaned from their mother too soon,
in nature's elements on the land,
under the sun, stars and moon.

Some cowboys, they did their best,
others sacrificed their health,
by selling their horses dignity and soul,
to entertain their own wealth.

Cavalry and order,
corruption, war and theft,
a new rule when training,
we must do everything on the left.

For years this was the law,
the only way it should be done,
a chief's prayer has been reborn,
mother nature has won.

If possible, perhaps the horses
would smile and be joyous,
man has found the old path again,
to return their dignity, *little fuss.*

Majestic and innocent,
yet so fragile, our friend the Equus,
a servant of the earth,
a living being and a right to *equal us.*

The Fox Hunt

All horses and hounds alert,
when the horn blows!
The chase is on, where to?
Nobody *bloody* knows!

Illegal is the sport,
everybody is on edge.
A fox runs for it is life,
as a horse is whipped *over* a hedge.

The law stated clearly
that live fox hunts were banned!
They ignored it because animal rights
in their mind *do not* stand.

Their other way around it
was to capture the red fiend.
Then instead release him later,
claiming he had not just been *freed*.

'He was simply in the way' they say,
'the dogs picked up the scent!'
'Can't tell em to stop you see,
they will not listen or relent!'

Drag hunts are an option,
but of course this will not do.
Blood-lust is their poison,
as is destroying the land they run *through*.

The Golden Surprise

Inspired by Chapter 5 of Zoë's award winning book
www.thehorsethatbroketwolegs.com.

Charismatic,
pure golden charm,
one need not
twist back my arm.

For me it was only
love at first sight,
already so familiar,
it just felt so right.

First eye contact from him
had a whirlwind effect,
wild in his heart
yet truly willing to connect!

He was already mine
as I hoped I was for him,
to me he was perfection
from ear to hind-limb.

Indeed it turns out
we were meant to be together,
our language and communication
is as light as a *feather*.

He is my mirror,
but also has a mind of his own,
together we are one,
never do we feel *alone*.

For I am,
I and he is he,
a kinship has formed forever
and true love is the key.

The Herd

Swift, agile and fast,
yet steady in their race,
following the leader,
complimenting each other's pace!

The dynamics are astounding,
when one observes galloping herds,
comparable to the formation,
of a flock of starling *birds!*

Sometimes sub-groups split
and head in another direction,
don't be fooled, they know what they are doing,
a temporary *disconnection.*

They soon reconnect,
shoulder to shoulder or nose to tail,
a silent communication,
a guarantee they shall prevail.

When the run is over
and the herd starts to slow,
the sound of hooves is lightened
and replaced by a nostril out blow.

Their breathing is rapid;
satisfaction radiates the atmosphere,
munching of grass starts to echo
as they come to a *standstill*.

The odd whiney or squeal can be heard,
just a clearing of a space,
communicated immediately,
where at worst some give chase!

A beautiful thing to witness,
especially if they do it just for pleasure,
freedom like that in today's world
really is a mindful treasure.

The Impolite Observer

Please do not observe my office
and tell me or my student what to do,
to make yourself feel better
from a glimpse of a minute or two!

There are a million ways
to teach something at any given time,
my student, the horse and what I am teaching,
really is just fine.

Come back in a year when things are better
and have fallen into place,
any critique I ask not during my lesson,
but after and too my face.

Finally, please make-sure you are perfect
in everything you do,
even though that is not possible anyway,
because remember it's not me *that* judged you!

The Instructor

An excellent instructor
knows how to give you a good feeling,
it is not their job to upset you
or leave any student reeling.

Timing is of an essence
to get things good and right,
to teach the rider lightness
and not get in a fight!

It is important that they study
and continue to do so,
maintaining their knowledge
and a good working flow!

With horses you see,
there is so much to learn,
trust and respect on both sides,
the good instructor must earn.

So if you have an instructor,
that displeases your ear,
for goodness sake find a new one,
so things *can* become more clear!

And if that's still not working,
they might not be the prob*lem*,
take a good look in the mirror,
it's very possible it is not just *them*.

The Lucky Fall

Be still my friend,
it can happen to us all,
lay there quietly for a minute,
to contemplate your fall.

Let those around you help,
the horse is probably okay,
listen to your instinct,
for a moment you must stay.

There is no shame in falling
from a live animal,
especially if you landed
on a jump, a floor or a *wall!*

In a few days' time,
when you are over your injury,
think about how to prevent that again
and become a better *me.*

Everything is an experience;
don't let anyone tell you different,
perhaps if they do,
it is because they have not experienced *it!*

You see my dear horse riding,
it is *not* a game,
they are decision making beings,
they also have a name.

They are not stupid, are smart,
quite intelligent in fact,
they respond to what we teach them
and can also simply over *react.*

The Mounted Archer

She draws back,
arrow set on her thumb,
her horses ear flickers,
ready for what's to *come.*

Her line of sight is clear,
the bow and arrow are steady,
the horse understands the pace needed,
habitually gallant and ready.

She hits the target with integrity,
mostly on a bulls-eye,
already drawing her new arrow,
ready for the next *fly-by.*

The Mustang

Hey ha hey, hey ha hey ho
Hey ha hey, he ya hey ho

I hear the drum

Dum

Dum

Dum

A call of the wolf echoes

His eye twinkles

Skin twitching at a fly

Breathing is shallow

Mains knotted and long

He stamps his hoof

Tail swishing side-to-side

Peaceful yet ready

Muscles tort and trained

Heart pumping slowly

Equipped to be afraid

His lips lick and chew

Muzzle is soft

Ears like radars

Always ready

Listen

Dum

Dum

Dum

The Obsession

It is so
They exist
Indefectible
Splendid
I admire
A fixation
Forever
The horse

The Obsolete Horse

I see you,
but you don't see me,
I hear you,
but you don't hear me,
I beg you to stop and listen,
what am I trying to say?
Darn it predator,
I just want to run away.

The Old Horse

Eyes of wisdom,
you can only hope from good fortune,
a fair life treated well,
with few visits to the veterinary *surgeon!*
Body and joints are not as agile
as they once were,
movement is more difficult
with stiff legs and achy *shoulder.*
More rest is required
and time to digest her food,
slower at everything,
but consistent in her mood!
The best outcome,
for this precious and loyal friend,
is how I wish for her life
to come to an end!
Perhaps laying down one night
in a cosy bed of straw,
her breath giving out painlessly,
as heaven quietly opens up a *door.*

The Pasture

I adore listening to the sound,
of their crunch and munch,
pastures green, for them,
breakfast, dinner, and *lunch*.
Sometimes their tail strikes,
swiftly at a fly,
or they stand doing nothing,
content with a sigh.
Playtime is fun,
perhaps picking up a gallop,
enduring dominance games,
to see who is top *rank*.
Or rolling in the mud,
flipping from side-to-side,
then gallantly trotting
with their friends at high stride!
The best part about these
precious moments watching them,
is their choice to leave it behind and come
when I call out their *name!*

The Pleasant Sacrifice

For the love of the horse,
that's why we do it,
learning everything about them
from nutrition to the bit!

Sunrise to moonrise
we have dedicated our lives,
to help the horses, the children,
the husbands and their wives!

Not often do we have much money,
many hours are unpaid,
a slave to our addiction;
an easy *overtrade!*

Probably the hardest part,
about what we do,
is less time with our own,
because we are spending it with you!

Our families, housework
and walking the dog in the park,
these things happen of course,
only not *until* long after dark.

Then as the sun rises,
it starts all over again,
one look at them is enough,
it really does keep us *sane.*

The Prison

Hidden away
from prying eyes,
a place to ignore
your silent cries.

Four walls, a ceiling
and a floor,
confined in prison,
can't open the door.

Perhaps time passes faster
when eating your food,
where minutes feel like hours,
dimming your mood.

When the night comes,
the only option is to rest,
enduring your wish to escape,
always doing your best.

When the day finally arrives,
you wait for the usual routine,
of food to pass the time again
and a glimpse of what could have *been*.

A dream of a choice to run,
dance, play and roll,
kicking out the way you should,
to feed the goodness of your soul.

Frolicking and bickering,
sliding in the mud,
getting dirty, creating havoc,
just like a young stud.

But alas,
this is not what could have been,
the ignorance dimming your cries
is not allowing it to be seen.

Hang in there my friend,
changes we are trying to make,
we think only of you
and the best for your sake.

The Ride

Long and vigorous neck,
connection to the mind,
haunches carry me,
no greater power I will find.

The back and spine move freely,
such a gift to be up here,
in full gallop an adrenaline rush,
I smile from ear to ear.

Every single time I ride,
I treasure the significance,
an animal carrying me on its back,
such a gift, what *magnificence!*

The Rival

Do not compare yourself,
to my horse or me,
I have no place
for competitiveness or *jealousy*.

Maybe your feeling
is that I know nothing,
it's really okay because
I know I know *something*.

That includes my own experience,
study and passion,
I do not do what I do,
to match the latest *fashion*.

Your thoughts about me are yours
and yours alone,
my thoughts about me are mine
and from this I have *grown*.

The Round Pen

A special space,
not only for lunging,
to create a language,
not just mindless *running.*

Often misused,
a place most horses hate,
twisting and turning too hard,
from timing that is *too late.*

By understanding some dynamics,
of how the horse's body and mind work,
life-changing things can be achieved,
quite the opposite of sending them *berserk.*

Don't chase them in circles,
nagging at their every stride,
give them a job, help them learn
and fill their hearts with solemn pride.

The Servant

Our friends, the serving horses,
front line and armed forces!

Postal service and transport,
most wars they have *fought.*

Then there is….

Farming and fox hunting,
Dressage and *show-jumping!*

A little child's dream,
market day where man is mean.

Big money at the races,
some travelled to distant places!

Worked hard, broken will,
many cultures do it still.

Wild horses no more,
not what the land is for.

As the grounds shrink,
100 years perhaps *extinct.*

A planet that's overran,
yep, just another legacy of man.

The Shetland

Oh how funny is this character
with his short and sturdy little body,
he does not *know* he is so small
and thinks he's as tall as *everybody*.

His neigh is simply priceless,
the cutest I ever heard,
to some horses he is scary,
you would think that quite *absurd*.

He does not hang about
and knows just what he wants,
can drag his human no problem,
to the green grass *restaurants!*

An asset to the equine family,
their name is known world-wide,
the most awesome little ponies,
for many a memory of their first ride.

The Sport

I question the strap,
so tight around your nose,
held firmly in place
to fake some shape or pose.

I question the relentless kicking
at your ribs and side,
forwards and *bloody* backwards
for some sort of ride.

I question the hands that jerk
and pull at your mouth,
in all the wrong directions,
but mostly too deep south!

I question the whip,
that burns at your skin,
a punishment or aid,
a game you can't win.

Finally I must question
the age old ego of man,
rosette, trophy or points,
doing *what* they think they can!

All riders and trainers
and experts of the jury,
open your heart, open your eyes,
I question....*what do you really see?*

The Trailer

Stand at the back of a double trailer,
what do you see?
I see two eyes, a mouth and a tongue,
staring back at me.

For the horse it is a trap,
no obvious way out,
every right to be concerned,
carrying a feeling of undue *doubt.*

Time must be taken
to teach them it is okay,
there are many ways to do it,
but fighting *is not* the way.

Watch those who succeed and whose horse,
hunts to go in the trailer,
ask them if they can help you,
to prevent a future disaster or a *failure.*

The biggest mistake people repeat
and do not seem to learn from,
is making the horse go in, closing it up
and hitting the road *again*.

At some point every horse will question,
do I really have to go in,
it's these moments the devil of the human,
sets out in mortal sin.

Don't be that person by leaving
your practice way too late,
teach them to load and be comfortable
and to learn how to rest and wait.

The Witness

Walk over, speak-up,
please don't just stand there,
use your voice, the horse cant,
rather than just stare.

It is time to walk the talk
and practice what we preach,
an example for our children,
let's change what we teach.

Was the horse whipped too hard,
or forced into Rollkur at a show,
we can help by saying something
and change what they think they know.

There is no need to be mean,
go about it with some wit,
ask them indirectly
why they are *doing it.*

Don't be surprised of course
if they do become offended,
give them nothing to oppose
and that no fight is *intended*.

Unless they continue
and they horse is suffering,
then do please say more,
to help stop the *abusing*.

It might not resolve everything,
but at least you had your say,
a pebble in the water,
sending a ripple the right way.

Them

Their eyes, their ears, their nose, their touch,
thoughts like ours, not so much.

Their long manes, such silken hair,
and mesmerizing cosmic stare!

With Mother Nature in their heart,
most predators, they can out-smart.

Their tail so long, protection from the flies,
a brain so small, no room for lies!

Man's soul can change in their presence,
fair trade for love, a natural *balance!*

For every step they shall make,
ones love for them, you cannot fake.

Think

Think about your questions
and what you are trying to teach,
they do not always understand you,
especially your speech.

Think about how difficult it is
when *you* learn new things,
it's not easy takes practice
and sometimes your ego it stings.

Think about the fact
that they are not here just for you,
if it's partnership you seek,
you have to offer it too.

Think about their intelligence,
it's not the same as us,
most are kind enough to offer things,
knowingly with *selflessness.*

Think about why you love them,
was it your heart they initially stole,
because I believe they were put on this earth
to play that very role.

To my Students

Of course it is not easy,
doing what I do,
I contemplate constantly
and mostly about you.

You *are* all I think about,
day and night,
questioning how can we get better,
did I tell them right?

But please do not worry;
I am satisfied in what I do,
my love to share knowledge about them,
I learn from it too.

There is no better feeling,
of witnessing your smile,
an acknowledgment of a feeling,
perhaps not felt in a while.

But also for your horses,
to see them understand,
I only change the thoughts in you
and your predatory hand.

To not share the secrets,
is a waste of history,
no point in keeping all of it,
just for my horse *and me.*

So please bear with me,
if I cannot always smile,
perhaps I was thinking about,
other stuff in that while.

Or maybe I have further things,
going on in my life,
I am after all a human being,
a daughter, sister and a wife.

Sometimes I have a great day
and others may appear not to be,
it's just because I think of you
and sometimes I have to think of me.

Thank you for your trust;
you love your horses just as much as I,
we all do our best each day;
we all laugh, smile and cry.

I promise you from this day forth,
to be the best of resources,
for you, my husband, my family
and for all our beloved *horses!*

Types

Arabians, Thoroughbreds,
Shetlands to Halflingers,
Black, Brown, White or a mix,
not forgetting the *Appaloosa's!*

Small, short and stocky,
also very wide,
big, tall or long,
all a great ride.

Hot blood, cold blood
and warm blood too,
ridden Western or English
also by the *Sioux!*

Short stride, long stride
and also medium,
to Show-jumping and Dressage,
in a *stadium!*

So many to choose from,
a variety to love,
much more diversity,
than all of the above!

Why not

Why would you want to train them
any other way?
when you can ride, run by their side
and also learn how to play.

Traditional methods are questioned,
their numbers are starting to decline,
stuff that is so old it is new again
has been reinstated to the *frontline.*

The way we look and act around horses
is changing by the year,
from S-line saddles to anatomic bridles
and brain saving head gear.

An obvious confusion,
is the discovery made by a new horse owner,
from a riding school, trained the old way,
they often feel like a loner.

Solely because times are changing,
things are moving ahead real fast,
those not willing to adjust their ways just yet,
will find themselves in trouble and probably last.

Winter

I adore their fluffy coats;
they look so different to the summer time,
some are wrapped in blankets
and some are left to bare the temp *decline.*

Neither is bad, as long as it is done
and thought out well,
with ad-lib food, water and a shelter
and not locked too often in a cell.

For millions of years they have subsisted,
they outlived the dinosaur,
they do not feel the same chill that you feel,
when you first step out your *door.*

Sure thing they feel the wind
and when the rain falls they identify,
not all of them seek shelter though,
but rather stay out not keeping *dry.*

When the snow falls,
they seek a frolic and a game,
or paw at the ground looking for food,
for them it's all the same.

Worrying about them too much
is waste of your mindful freedom,
just wrap yourself up nice and warm,
so you can enjoy them this winter *season*.

About the Author

Zoë was born at the Royal London Hospital in the East of London, Great Britain in 1975.

In 2005 after growing up with horses in the suburbs and countryside of Essex, she moved to Haarlem, the Netherlands to settle down with her husband.

For many years she stayed away from home and prides herself in still doing so; to study with some of the best Horsemen and women all over the world.

A Horse Professional, Instructor, Trainer and Coach since 2007, she teaches many subjects in cooperation with the true nature of the horse. These include; problem solving, young horse starting, trailer loading, Liberty, trick training, general habits and skills right through to show-jumping, cross country, rehabilitation and the Academic Art of Riding.

In 2017 she participated as a trainer at the Mustang Makeover in Aachen, Germany. A first of its kind event in Europe!

That same year she published her debut book titled: *the horse that broke two legs & survived* in three languages; English (original) Dutch and German. In 2018 the book won Best Non-Fiction and her poem titled: *The Equus* won Best International Poem at the EQUUS Film Festival in New York, USA.

Earlier that year she was approached by a movie Director/Producer to contribute her thoughts and star in the Award Winning documentary titled: *Listening to the Horse – The Movie.*

She also starred alongside long term friend and mentor Eddy Modde *(eddie lives)* in his International Award Winning song and music video called *Horse Reflections.*

Currently Zoë continues to influence the horse community and can be found sharing her success, passion and knowledge on Facebook and Instagram.

www.zoecoade.com/books

Zoë Coade - Equestrian Author & Poet

zoecoade

the horse that *broke* two legs & survived

A biographic compilation of true events from both past to present day portrays the inspirational life of one determined lady and her cherished but troubled horse.

Often referring to the big and powerful mount as her professor she shares with you their distinct journey and how the horse survived and healed two broken legs.

Amazon.co.uk /.com
Paperback / Kindle

Het paard dat twee benen *brak* & overleefde

Een biografische compilatie van ware gebeurtenissen uit het verleden tot de dag van vandaag vertelt het verhaal van het inspirerende leven van een vastberaden vrouw en haar geliefde maar beproefde paard.

Vaak refererend aan het grote en krachtige rijpaard als haar professor, deelt ze met jou haar bijzondere reis en hoe het paard twee gebroken benen overleefde.

Amazon.nl / Bol.com
Kindle / Paperback

Das Pferd, das sich zwei Beine *brach* und es überlebte

Eine biografische Beschreibung wahrer Ereignisse porträtiert das inspirierende Leben einer willensstarken jungen Frau und ihres geliebten, aber mit Problemen belasteten Pferdes, von der Vergangenheit bis heute.

Sie lässt Sie teilhaben an ihrer besonderen gemeinsamen Reise und beschreibt, wie dieses große, starke und tapfere Pferd, das von ihr liebevoll als ihre „Professorin" bezeichnet wird, zwei Beinbrüche erlitt und diese überlebte.

Amazon.de
Taschenbuch / Kindle

Printed in Great Britain
by Amazon

74402201R00073